FINANCE
Budgeting

Save Money, Invest for Retirement and Get Debt Free

By Andrew W. Welch

Andrew W. Welch

Andrew W. Welch

author or copyright owner. Legal action will be pursued if this is breached.

Disclaimer Notice:

Please note the information contained within this document is for educational and entertainment purposes only. Every attempt has been made to provide accurate, up to date and reliable complete information. No warranties of any kind are expressed or implied. Readers acknowledge that the author is not engaging in the rendering of legal, financial, medical or professional advice.

Table of Contents

Introduction

All of us race behind money to attain "financial success". But what exactly is financial success? Is it about having more assets to your name? Is it about having no debts? Or is it about having more savings? Or is it a lucrative investment portfolio? The perception of financial success varies from person to person.

But what is the one common factor that drives you towards this financial success? Allow me to introduce you to the concept of budgeting. It does not matter if your definition of financial success differs from that of your friend's for the both of you can use the tool of budgeting to achieve this success. In simple words, budgeting is the process of being aware of your income and expenses. This knowledge helps you in taking conscious financial decisions. This is precisely why the concept of budgeting is very important.

We have all applied the concept of budgeting in some way or the other in our lives. For instance, when we go out for a movie, we tend to spend within what we have in hand. This is a simple example of a mini budget. This, when extrapolated, becomes your budget for the month. We all budget without really knowing its many benefits. However, that is about to change now.

In this book, I have given you an overview of budgeting and its many benefits in the first chapter. In the second chapter, I have listed out certain tips to budgeting for beginners. Common mistakes one should avoid while budgeting is mentioned in the third chapter while the fourth chapter addresses the common questions you might have in connection with budgeting.

I hope you find it an engaging and informative read. Thank you for purchasing this book.

Chapter 1: Introduction to Budgeting

In this chapter, let us look at what budgeting is and why we should regard budgeting seriously.

What is budgeting?

A budget is nothing but an estimate of one's income and expenses in a given period. In other words, budgeting is a tool used to manage your finances. This may be both short term as well as long term in nature.

Let us look at the two fundamental components of a budget now.

Income:

Identify the different sources from which you earn every month. Most of us earn incomes from more than one source. These sources include salaries, wages, profits earned from business, investment income, rental income etc. When you make a list, at the beginning of a month, of the amount you would be earning from the various sources, you will have a clear idea of the quantum of money you would have in hand to take of all your expenses for the month. There are also passive and portfolio investments to account for and make sure you write down every income that there is to.

Expenses:

We incur expenses for various reasons in a given month. When you write down all the expected expenses, you will be prepared to face them. Never disregard any expense as trivial. If you make several trivial payments in a month, the aggregate would be a tidy sum. Make sure you note all of them down. Some of the categories of expenses that we incur on a monthly basis are as follows:

> ➤ Household bills: This comprises of your mortgage, electricity, water, rent and grocery expenses. You will have to keep your bills handy in order to make a note of the expenses.

> ➤ Financial Products: Expenses pertaining to financial products are nothing but the cost involved pertaining to your investments such as brokerage, commission fees etc. It also includes the premium that you pay on your insurance and medical plans every month.

> ➤ Family and friends: These include the expenses incurred in connection with your family and friends. At the

beginning of every month, list the upcoming anniversaries, birthdays, baby showers etc. This way you will know how much to set aside for these events.

➤ Travel: Travel expenses include the amount of money you spend on gas every month. In case, you don't own a car, this will include the amount you spend on bus rides, metro and cab rides in a month. Apart from this, if you have planned to leave town sometime during the month, then make note of the expenses that you might have to incur from the travel, to and fro.

➤ Leisure: The money you spend on entertainment (such as movies, theatre), dinners and other expenses incurred in connection with leisure activities are clubbed under this category.

➤ Miscellaneous expenses: If you incur any expenses that do not fall under the above heads, they can be clubbed under miscellaneous expenses.

➤ Contingent expenses: The reason why we struggle a lot financially is because we do not take into consideration the contingency expenses that may come our way. Contingent expenses are nothing but the expenses that you anticipate in a given month. Learn to set aside a portion of your income every month to meet your contingent expenses. Since these are more anticipatory than actual in nature, you can carry forward this contingent fund to the next month if it was not used up this month. This way, you will be prepared to face any emergency expenses that might come your way.

Benefits of budgeting:

We often neglect budgeting as we regard it as a tedious task. However, this will change once you know the different benefits of budgeting. The following are some of the important benefits of having a budget in hand and following it religiously.

> ➤ **Control over your money**

We often run behind money all the time and end up being controlled by money. However, the opposite happens when you have a budget in hand. When you have a budget, you end up controlling your money. You will know exactly how much you earn and spend. This information can save you a lot of stress. For instance, when you have a clear idea of your income and expenses, you will know the amount left for repaying if you have intentions of borrowing. Often we borrow money keeping only our incomes in mind as opposed to taking a holistic view. This will help us understand our repaying capacity and handle debt in an organized way.

Apart from the control over your money, you will also be prepared even for the worst-case scenario.

➤ **Focus on our money goals**

All of us have different financial goals. For some of us, our financial goals are aimed at settling our debts. For others, it is about increasing our assets. For few others, it is about increasing the quantum of savings. Other financial goals include preparing for retirement, increasing income from the different sources, having a prosperous investment portfolio etc. Budgeting helps you in attaining your financial goals easily. This is because, with a budget in hand, you earn and spend with the desired goal in mind. Your goals can be both short term and long term in nature. As long as you have financial goals to attain you will find that your budgets have come in handy. With this focus, you will be able to achieve your financial goals sooner than you think.

➤ **Makes you aware what is going on with your money**

We often wonder what happened to all the money we earned, when we become broke in the middle of the month. We keep thinking where all the money went. Say no to these shocking epiphanies by formulating a budget. When you have a budget in hand, you will be able to keep a track on what comes in and what goes out. We will also be able to track those expenses that we had failed to include in the first place and include it in the subsequent budgets. In fact, budgets are mandatory for those who have the habit of spending unnecessarily on unwanted things. Imagine how much peace you will have if you know exactly where all your money went. You won't have to sit down and pressurize your brain to remember that things you bought. You will know exactly where it went and not repent having blown it off on unwanted things.

> ➤ **Organizing your expenditure and savings**

When we actually analyze the amount that we spend for different purposes, we will realize that a major portion of it is spent for useless reasons. We have the habit of spending on things that we don't really need for various reasons. How often have we purchased so many things because they were cheap or bought a piece of furniture because our neighbor bought it even if we didn't need it? Since we don't keep a tab on our expenses, we don't realize how much of our money gets spent on redundant stuff. A budget helps us in identifying these unnecessary expenses and helps us to cut down on them.

When we spend judiciously, we are left with more money to save. One of the hindering factors to increases savings is the never-ending list of expenses. With organized expenditure, your quality and quantum of savings will also improve.

➢ **Contingency expenditure**

As mentioned earlier, one of the important reasons for financial stress is because we don't plan for unforeseen expenses. With a budget in hand, we are prepared to meet even the unforeseen expenses, if we set aside a sum every month on a contingent basis. This fund could reduce your stress drastically should you run into any emergency, which can be both financial and medical in nature. It might not occur in your immediate family alone and if an emergency arises in your extended family then you can save the day and provide financial help to those in need and remain happy and proud. Make sure you start saving for the emergency again if you have exhausted it on something.

➢ **Identifying potential commitments**

Although we begin preparing a budget for a month, we soon begin to prepare budgets for the long term as well. When you develop this habit, you will realize how a certain expense you make in a given month is impacting your expenses after six months. For instance, if you are intending to purchase a car this month, then you can expect to incur expenses for gas.

Similarly, it helps you in preparing for a future commitment such as the repayment of a debt, which is due after six months. We generally tend to work on such a repayment only when the deadline nears. When you have a budget in hand, you start saving for this debt from tomorrow as opposed to after five months. This way, this repayment will not burn a hole in your pocket.

> **Increase your income**

A budget helps not only in managing your expenses but also in increasing your income. When we take a note of the amount left after taking care of all our expenses, we can think of ways to use this money to increase our income. One way to increase our income would be to save the money and earn interest on it. An alternate solution would be to invest the money on shares or other securities and earn dividend on them. This way, you can multiply your existing income with less effort.

➢ **Determines your debt appetite**

As mentioned earlier, we tend to borrow money without taking into consideration our monthly commitments. This is why debts intimidate us. When you prepare a budget, you will know what portion of your income is left after taking care of all expenses that can be used for repayment. Based on this, you can borrow accordingly as you will be able to commit a fixed sum every month towards the repayment.

➢ **Debt management**

When we have several debts, a budget helps us in prioritizing them and repaying them within the stipulated time. Our debts can be classified into two categories namely priority debts and non-priority debts. As the name suggests, the consequence of failure of repayment of priority debts will have serious repercussions that make it prudent to repay them immediately. List down their deadlines and apportion a sum towards their repayment every month when you formulate your budget. In other words, a sound budget will help you in dealing with your debts effectively.

➢ **Peaceful Retirement**

As mentioned earlier, budgets can be prepared for long term as well. Preparing a budget for your retirement years will help you in identifying what will be the income you will be earning after retirement and the expenses that you might incur, after taking into consideration the rates of inflation. When you prepare a budget for your retirement, you will know how much you will need after retirement to lead a hassle free life. You can start saving for it accordingly starting from today. That way, your life after retirement is taken care of. In fact, if you have planned it well enough then you can retire early and lead a happy and content life. You don't have to force yourself to go to work, which can really get tiring if you are almost reaching your retirement age.

➤ **Spread the message**

This means that you have a chance to teach your children and other people around you the importance of being on a budget and saving money on a monthly basis. It is important for your children to imbibe the habit and start saving as early as possible. If they begin saving money from their daily allowance then with time, they might have enough to pay for their college. Similarly, if you have a sibling or a spouse that you wish to inspire into taking up budgeting then you can set an example for them to follow.

These are some of the various benefits of budgeting. As you might have noticed, effective and consistent budgeting will help in increasing your savings, improving your investment portfolio, managing your debts effectively and prepare for your retirement peacefully.

Andrew W. Welch

Chapter 2: Tips for Budgeting

If you are a beginner to budgeting, then the pointers suggested in this chapter will definitely help you out. These pointers will not only helping you to formulating a budget but also sticking to it. I have also listed out some budgeting tools that can assist you with this.

Budgeting tips:

One of the important aspects of budgeting is reducing your expenses. Half the time, we tend to cross our budgets because we end up spending more than we anticipated. Hence, I have mentioned some pointers pertaining to the reduction of expenses in this chapter.

Learn to be flexible

It is certain that we will not be able to follow our budget exactly. This is because; sometimes our expenses may be more than what we expected. Hence the key is to have a liberal mindset when you formulate your budget. This way, you will be in a safe place even when met with the worst-case scenario. On the contrary, if you have a conservative budget, you tend to become flustered if your expenses exceed the budget. So try and leave a little money as an emergency fund for your monthly expenses. This amount should be utilized only for your emergency expenses and not be used for anything else. Don't go to this money if you are trying to buy something over and above your monthly needs and after fulfilling your monthly luxury needs. This is for those times that you really have to make an urgent purchase such as a laptop because your old one suddenly went kaput. So be prepared for any type of emergency and remain flexible with your budget.

Make room for some fun

All work and no fun make every day dull. Similarly, a budget that does not take into consideration the expenses you might have to incur in connection with having fun is a boring one. When you don't make room for your leisure activities in your budget, you will feel frustrated after spending money on such activities. A conservative budget is not going to stop us from having fun. We might as well plan for these expenses instead of regretting after spending. Moreover, when we set aside a sum every month for fun activities, we will be able to have fun in an organized fashion. You will see in the sample budget that entries such as "leisure time" and "club" money have been added in. these are important for everyone. You cannot stop socializing just because you have to stick to a budget. You need to entertain yourself in order to function properly. There are many people who will not add these charges to their budget thinking it will get adjusted. But nothing will get adjusted unless you consciously adjust it. So these charges are mandatory to be added into your monthly budget.

Spend below your income

Never spend more than what you earn. We tend to borrow and spend sometimes. Repayments of these debts become a problem next. This has to be borne in mind if you use a credit card to purchase things. Never exhaust the limit and buy more. This will increase the rate of interest associated with the card as well. Hence never spend over and above your income. If you have that kind of problem, then start taking a friend along so that they can stop you from making unnecessary purchases. You need to take with you your prepared budget everywhere you go so that you know how much you need to spend on something and where you need to curb your spending. If you think you are on the verge of over spending then consciously stop yourself and say to yourself, I will buy this next month.

Borrow for the right reasons

Borrow only if it is used to finance a long-term investment. This way, your asset will help you in repaying the debt incurred. For instance, if you take an education loan, you will be able to repay the loan from the income you earn because of your qualification. Similarly, if you invest in a house, you will be able to repay the loan from the rental income you are earning. Avoid borrowing for reasons that will not benefit you with the passage of time. For instance, you borrow money to buy a car. The value of the car depreciates over time and such an investment is not profitable if you are making it in the first place with a loan. Similarly, you decide to borrow to go on a lavish holiday. Once you are done with it, you are left with a big headache to pay the loan on time. So choose not to borrow for something that won't pay big over time and you are sure of having a good chance at making the money and paying off the debt duly.

Rent

Never wait till the first of every month to pay your rent. If you do have enough money before the beginning of the next month, pay off your rent instead of waiting for the first. You should do this without fail if you have any apprehensions of spending the money before the first of the upcoming month. Defaulting in the payment of your rent is something that you can easily avoid. If you do default then you will be troubles of all sorts. You will have to live with bad credit and might also get kicked out. These are problems you don't need especially if you are just starting out with your career.

Overpay your mortgage

It is not necessary that you have to pay only the stipulated amount towards your mortgage every month. If during any month, you have extra money, pay more than what is required for the mortgage. This way, you will be able to close it sooner and reduce the interest component. So choose to pay at least 10% more than you usually would in a month towards your mortgage. You can choose a bigger number as well if you think it will be easier for you to pay off your mortgage by contributing 15% extra than normal towards it. You need to come up with a good plan in order to do this.

Utilities

Invest in power saving utilities such as fluorescent bulbs. These reduce your electricity bill to a greater extent. Adjust the temperature of the thermostat to reduce your cooling and heating costs. Usage of ceiling fans will also help in reducing your electricity bill. These utilities are a onetime investment that can save a lot of expenses in the future. Hence apportion a part of your budget to take care of these expenses.

Transportation expenses

Plan to finish multiple errands in a single trip. This way, you can reduce the fuel consumption and thereby reduce the money spent on gas. This is also an effective way to manage your time.

Budgeting utilities:

Use one of the following systems to keep a tab on your money and follow your budget:

Notebook and pen

As simple as this may seem, sometimes all you need is a notebook and a pen to write down all your incomes and expenses. You can also maintain a separate column for the savings you make. Though these are least expensive ways of keeping track of your money, the risk of misplacing the notebook is always there. When you decide to sit down and prepare your budget just make sure that you have these handy and are not simply sitting down being unprepared for it or scamper at the last minute to find these.

Spreadsheet

Your simple looking excel can work wonders. This also helps in avoiding manual errors and you will be able to perform even complex calculations in a matter of seconds and get the most accurate figure. The best thing about using the spreadsheet is that once you set the formula for certain fields, you don't have to rework the entire thing even if you change the figures. So start by making a conclusive excel sheet for your budget and use it on a monthly basis to simply change the values in it. You can save a copy of it on all your devices and also mail it to yourself. The final goal is to have it ready on a monthly basis in order to quickly fill in the details and prepare the budget with ease.

Financial Software

There are several financial softwares available out there such as Microsoft money and Quicken. These are a complex version of your spreadsheet and are capable of tracking your income and expenses in a better way. This helps you to keep a tab on your investment accounts and bank accounts as well. You will have a chance to look all your accounts and know how much money you have and where. However, this is risky if someone else gains access to your computer. They will be able to access details of your finances in a jiffy.

Online Software

These days, you have different versions of online software that help you track your money and monitor your budget. Most of these are free while the others come at a minimal cost. As they are web based, you will be able to access the figures from anywhere.

You will be able to update your expenses immediately without any delay. You can directly link all your bank accounts and have them unified. You will have a chance at tracking your expenses and won't have to roam around with a pen and paper. You will have everything at your fingertips and can easily make modifications to anything and everything that is related to your budget and finances. However, not many people would be comfortable in updating their financial information online. There is the threat of fraud and also identity theft. So remain wary of such dubious websites and choose something that is completely trustworthy and has a good reputation so that your money and identity are safeguarded. You can ask any of your friends for a suggestion to be safe.

Chapter 3: Basic Mistakes to Avoid In Budgeting

In this chapter, we have highlighted the common mistakes that need to be avoided while budgeting. If you take care of these common mistakes, then you are ready to say hello to a sound budget plan.

Forgetting to write down your expenses

Since it is not possible to completely follow our budgets, the only way we can perfect the upcoming budgets is by analyzing the present one and look at the deviations. These deviations are usually the additional expenses that we incur. Make sure you write down all your expenses as and when you incur them. Even if you are not able to update your budget immediately, do it before the end of the day. Don't forget to note them down. So it is always based on experience and trial and error. You cannot perfect your budget from the get go. You need to understand that various subtle things that can impact your budget in a big way. Don't forget to make note of the smaller adjustments, as they will also contribute towards raising your budget substantially.

Not writing down purchases

When we review our budget, we are indirectly keeping a track on our money. This analysis sometimes highlights the unnecessary purchases we have made during the month. Out of shame, we might not note these expenses intentionally. The whole point of budgeting is to ensure that we identify the redundant expenses and cut down on them. If you fail to note them down, they will never get tracked and you will start wondering where such a big chunk of money went. So even if it is a guilty pleasure like buying a toy for your collection, it is important to include it in your budget. Basically, count in everything that you think is an expense towards reducing your monthly income. Nobody will look at your budget to judge you and so, it is best that you remain as honest with it as possible.

Budget busters

In simple words, these refer to those expenses that are over and above the budgeted amount. If the difference is negligible, then it is not a matter of concern. However, if the difference is vast, then either watch what you spend next time or make room for such differences in your budget. As was said before, these might be small things that you think will not impact your budget in a big way but in reality, they will actually turn out to be big numbers. So don't take any expense for granted and account for everything that there is to. You will not think spending $4 on coffee a day will amount to a big number but expenses are always cumulative and over a period of time, you will realize you have lost a lot of money that you cannot even trace back.

Being conservative

One of the biggest mistakes when it comes to budgeting is being frugal. When you draw up a very conservative budget, you will obviously end up spending more than what you expected to spend. Since a frugal budget does not take into consideration any extravagant expenses, you will obviously end up spending outside the budget. The outcome of having a frugal budget is that you will feel frustrated for not following it properly. So try and include everything that you think you will incur on a monthly basis. A sample budget has been attached at the end of this chapter in order for you to understand how it works. Everything that a person might incur has been added in and it is best that you use it as a template to follow. An emergency amount has not been added in because adding one might tempt you to use it up and exhaust it by the end of the month. So it is important that you not add one at all and even if you do, you add in just $10 as the budget.

Not considering the time value of money

Often when we prepare budgets for long term, we forget to take the time value of money into consideration. Hence our budgets will not be completely accurate. Time value of money simply means that the value of ten dollars today is not same as the value of ten dollars after one year, given the inflation rate. Always take into consideration the time value of money when you are preparing a long-term budget such as planning for your retirement. You need to bear in mind how things used on a daily basis will be spiked up and must plan according to how much you will need in a month. Retirement savings are discussed in detail further in this book.

Sample budget for your reference

Sample budget

Monthly Income		Monthly Expenses	
Monthly Salary	$2,000		
Passive Income- Food Sales	$500	Personal Loans	$300
Portfolio Investments: Interests & Dividends	$500	Credit Card Charges	$400
		Utilities	$100
		Healthcare	$40
		Gas/Transportation	$100
		Food/Groceries	$160
		Singing Class	$60
		Personal Care	$40
		Clothing	$100
		Night out with Friends	$300
Total Income	$3,000	Total Payable	$2,0000
Total Income	$3,000		
(-) Total Expenses	$2,000		
Surplus	$1,000		

Remember that this is just an imaginary budget and yours might look different. You must prepare one that is true to your incomes and expenses. Don't leave out anything and if your expenses are surpassing your income then choose to adjust your budget and make the two match. If they are not matching then try and cut down on certain items like the singing class for a month or two until your finances stabilize. Once they do, you can rejoin these classes.

Chapter 4: Common Questions Pertaining To Budgeting

The word budgeting is often misunderstood by a huge percentage of the common populace outside of those who are in some way related to, or work in the finance field. However, this is something, that knowingly or unknowingly every man with a remote interest in saving his hard earned coins does at some level or the other. A decent knowledge about the core principles of budgeting will help you immensely in managing your finances.

In this chapter I shall list out some of the most common queries with respect to the concept of budgeting, which will aid you setting targets for the month, earmarking funds, paying off any debts or installments and managing the mortgage without it adversely affecting your liquidity.

Andrew W. Welch

What is the ideal amount to be marked for investments?

When it comes to ascertaining the amount of money to be set aside for investment, three factors are of paramount importance. They are age, disposable income and liquidity position. So let us take a look at all three of these, one by one.

- ➢ As you can imagine, the budgeting decisions and consequent investment tactics depend a lot on the age of the investor. In case of young people, the major factors to be considered include the future investment plans such as real estate purchases or buying residential spaces such as apartments etc. Since at the beginning of careers, the income may not be that high, the amount of money that can be put aside for these purposes will also be less.
- ➢ The next factor is disposable income. Essentially it is the amount that is left with you after meeting all the pressing needs and requirements in life. In an ideal scenario, it denotes the money that you have in hand after you have spent enough to pay all the bills and other unavoidable expenses. However there is a cache here. This disposable income can either be put away as savings for a rainy day, or it can be spent in acquiring the finer things in life by indulging in some luxuries.

❯   Liquidity position denotes the ease or viability of converting your non-cash assets into cash. This is highly important in terms of quantum of the proposed investment. It may be your own money, but if it blocked in some kind of set-up in which you are not allowed to access it before a certain period of time, then you are practically left without that money during such period of time.

One of the most convenient methods of saving up include going in for employer sponsored retirement accounts. These methods allow you to make use of pre-tax money for funding the investment. In this vein, let us answer one of the most frequently asked questions regarding investment; how much of the income to be invested! There is no steadfast answer for this, but a minimum of 10% of your net income will prove to be a tidy sum. Anything higher is always welcome as long as it doesn't leave you high and dry.

How much money should be kept aside for repayment?

The amount of money that should be kept aside of repayment of already existing loans depends to a large extent on the repayment schedule. There are some instruments that can be repaid only in accordance with the terms prescribed and then there are rolling debt instruments that let you pay them off based on your capabilities. Credit cards usually fall into the latter category.

But financial advisors and investment experts hold strong to one maxim here; that is to never invest money in taxable accounts when you have outstanding credit card balances. This is simply because of the reason that most credit card companies charge you anything between 5% and 30% as the annual interest rate, which is pretty much what you can hope to earn from the said investment. Hence it is always advisable to pay off one's dues before earmarking funds for investment in taxable accounts.

When it comes to repayment itself, some research can actually help you a lot here. Some credit agencies will be willing to alter the payment schedules if you request them to do so. Because many a time, we can see people who will be perfectly willing to pay more monthly, but will be tied down by the pre-decided terms and hence end up paying more as interest. In such cases, you can check whether it is possible to have the monthly repayment amount increased. But exercise caution while doing so, because there is something called "prepayment penalties" that may be attracted for repayment of a debt earlier than decided.

What about overpaying the mortgage?

The mortgage is another area where you can employ the method mentioned in the earlier section; that is overpaying. We do agree that in almost all normal cases, the mortgage will be the cheapest source of debt. But still if you can afford to pay more monthly, then very well do so.

But there are some prerequisites that have to be considered here. First and foremost, make sure that all high interest debt is settled completely before you decide to overpay the mortgage. Secondly, ensure that a security net is in place before you take this leap. By security net, what I meant is the creation of an emergency fund worth 2 or 3 months income. Another thing to keep in mind is that there should be no opportunity cost for the amount overpaid. That is, if you had not paid the extra, then the amount should only have gone to savings.

How to chalk out a budget and maintain it?

Preparation and maintenance of a budget is really no rocket science. Do it a few times and you will get the hang of it pretty well. But there are some key pointers to be kept in mind. During the first few months, the stress should be on reviewing the financial statements to ascertain how much money was spent under different heads of expenses. These actual figures should be compared against the figures that you had marked out in the budget. Accordingly the budget should be tweaked.

And then there is the issue of one-time expenses that will invariably crop up every now and then. These include expenses incurred for replacing some major part of your car or any appliance at home etc. It would be prudential to list these under some miscellaneous category instead of regular maintenance expenses, as these are by no means recurring.

You can also get your partner or spouse to prepare one in order to have company. A sibling will also do and the two of you can remind each other to prepare the monthly budget on time. Although most people prefer to prepare one at the beginning of the month, you can do yours at the end as well to remain prepared for the next month.

How to deal with expenses that don't fit anywhere?

As I had mentioned earlier, there will always be expenses that apparently do not fit under any head. Do not worry because this is the case with every budget. By now you must have realized that no budget is perfect and the process of budgeting itself is an ever-evolving, ever-correcting one.

Expenses that cannot be bought under any fixed or variable head should be mentioned under the miscellaneous head. The only thing to be ensured is that, at no point of time should your miscellaneous section show a huge figure as compared to the rest of the budget. This calls for recurrent and timely evaluation of your budget in order to keep it updated and equipped to deal with the varying nature of your finances. Remember, these expenses need to be regular ones and not something that come about once in a while. As long as it is a regular expense, you can add it under the miscellaneous heading.

Chapter 5: Debt Repayment Strategies

Most Americans have heavy debts to repay, owing to affording a car, house etc. The amount borrowed is usually quite high and they need to plan out how to repay their debts, at the earliest, in order to reduce the interest that these debts invite. There are two ways in which you can repay your debts and they are as follows.

You might pay off your debts little by little no doubt, but you need to pay them off in full at some point in time or the other. For this, you can choose between two debt repayment methods, viz. the snowball method and the avalanche method. Here is looking at the two methods in detail.

Snowball method

Also known as the smallest balance plan, the snowballing method is one where the lowest debts are paid first followed by the biggest ones. So you need to list out all your debts in such a way that you mention the lowest one on top followed by the rest. Remember to include the final amount that you owe after adding in the interest amount.

Advantages

The main advantage of choosing this method is that, you get a chance to repay all your small debts, which will add to your confidence. When you have a lot of debts, you will feel insecure and doubt whether you have the capacity to repay all of it. But once you start repaying and close the debt, your confidence levels will spike. You will develop the confidence to get done with all the debts and be in a position to pay off the bigger ones as well. Many Americans choose this method for its psychological effects. They think of it as a better choice owing to the confidence it leaves them with.

Disadvantages

The disadvantage of this method is that, you will have to deal with the bigger amounts later, which might grow in volume owing to high rate of interest charged by the creditors. So you might have to pay more than what you actually had initially, and end up with a bigger headache. So it pays to plan out how you wish to deal with your debts in advance. If you think your confidence will not dwindle then this is a good plan to start with. But if you fear losing your confidence owing to a large amount of money waiting to be paid then it is best that you consider the next type of debt repayment method.

Avalanche method

The other method that you can adopt to pay off your debts is the avalanche method. This is opposite to the snowball method. Also known as the largest balance plan method, the debtor repays the biggest debt first followed by the smallest one. So it is important to note down the big debts first followed by the small ones.

Once you have prepared the list, you must start paying the biggest debt first and move to the next once it has been fully repaid. Let us now look at this method's advantages and disadvantages.

Advantages

The main advantage of this method is that, you don't have to worry about the big debts at the end. You will have a chance to go back to normal life once the big debts have been paid for. You can then leisurely pay off the small debts and be done with it. As per experts, this method is better than the previous one in terms of a person's financial standpoint. He or she will have a chance to finish repaying all debt without incurring too much interest. With time, they will be able to pay off all their debts and not be stuck with unnecessary interest. However, experts also believe that people do not choose this method owing to the psychological affect that it has on them.

Disadvantages

The main disadvantage of this method is that, people have to come up with a large sum of money to pay off the biggest debts. Coming up with a large sum will discourage them and they might give up half way through. So they will not be in a position to pay off their debts on time, which will add to their woes. But it is important to understand that this method is preferable and that you need to consider the positives. You can try and borrow the money from someone and pay off the debts at the earliest. Here is what you can do to raise the money faster and stop the train of high interest from coming into your life.

Borrow from family

The best thing to do is to borrow from your family members. You can ask them to lend you some money that you can use to pay off your debts. Remember that your family members will still want their money back but you might not have to pay them a large interest. You can convince them to give it to you at a reasonable interest rate. Make sure you borrow the entire amount that needs to be repaid and pay it off as soon as you come into money. You can approach any relative you think will help you out and pay you the amount at the earliest.

Borrow from insurance money

Remember that you can always borrow some money from your insurance policy. That is, you can borrow money from your insurance and pay off your debts. But remember that you cannot forget about it and must repay the money. You might also be charged a small interest for it but it will still work to your advantage.

Borrow from another bank

Many times, you might have debts from a lot of places that will all invite different rates of interest. For this, you can choose to borrow a lump sum from one bank or financial institution that gives away a good and low rate of interest. You can then pay off all your debts and you won't have a problem in paying back the different debts one by one. But remember that you have to have a good credit score in order to do so. If you don't have one then you won't be able to make this move. Make sure you have a credit score that is above 500 or at least above 400 in order to remain in the safe zone.

Andrew W. Welch

Speak with creditors

Sometimes, it is a good idea to speak with the creditors and try and reduce the debt that you have to pay. This is next to impossible but if you have been paying all your debts on time and have just a little more left to repay then you can ask him or her to reduce the amount or lessen the rate of interest.

These form the two ways in which you can repay your debts and lead a normal life. You must take these up at some point in time and it is best that you do it straight away.

Chapter 6: Increasing Monthly Income

Remember that you need to pay off all your debts in time and for that to happen, raise as much money as possible at the earliest. So look for passive sources to earn something extra on a monthly basis. Here are ideas that you can put to use and make a few extra dollars on a monthly/ yearly basis.

Passive incomes

Passive incomes are those that you earn by not actively participating in the activity. These are activities that you take up to add to your monthly income. It might not be possible for you to take up all these and might have to take up only the most viable option.

Rent from property

If you have enough money to buy a house then don't waste time and do so at the earliest. You can earn a monthly rent from your house, which will supplement your regular income. It need not be a palatial house and you can look for something that is in good condition. Once you buy it, you can rent it out and utilize the rent to repay any of your loans. It might not be a good idea to buy a house by borrowing another loan unless you have planned it all out carefully.

You will always have the house for yourself and can sell it for a profit later. Until such time, you must profit out of it and try and raise enough money to pay off all your debts. You will also have tax benefits and end up saving quite a bit of money, which can all be redirected towards getting your debts paid in full at the earliest.

Writing jobs

If you have a flair for writing then you can consider taking up writing to earn a little money on a monthly basis. You can pen down a novel or a book on a subject of your expertise and sell it online. Every time someone buys your book, you get paid for it. So you can sell as many books as you like and choose a diverse group of topics to write on.

But remember, if you wish to make it big, you need to be as unique as possible and not give people what they already have. The competition is very stiff and you have to be careful about what you put out there for people to read. Don't emulate someone else and try and be as unique as possible.

You can also write content for others as a freelancer and look for jobs on the Internet. There are several publishing houses that will feature guest articles and you can try your luck by submitting something interesting to them. You will also have a chance to speak on a topic of your choice and raise your voice against an issue and get many people to read what you put out. You can then start a blog and gather a crowd.

Affiliate marketing

If you succeed in gathering a crowd for the content that you put out then you will have a chance to make it big with affiliate marketing. Affiliate marketing refers to tying up with companies to promote their products and services. So if the company thinks there are several people who will buy their products owing to you having a strong reader base, then they will approach you for a tie up or vice versa.

They will give you a set of links that you have to sprinkle all over your website and get people to click on it. Every time someone clicks on the link and buys the product after being redirected from your website, you get paid for it. But you need to be a good salesman and provoke people into clicking on the link. If they simply continue reading and don't buy any products then you won't get paid. So it is best to publicize that you have a tie up and them clicking on it will aid in you continuing with your blog and them getting to read it for free. It is possible for you to make up $1000 or more depending on how well you write and promote a certain product.

Gardening

Gardening is a hobby that is dear to several people. If you have a lot of plants that produce flowers, vegetables and fruits, consider selling them in the market and making money. If you are already self sufficient with your produce then consider planting a few more plants and selling the produce in the market. Although you might not break into huge profits soon enough, you will be in a good position within a year or two.

Once you develop the confidence to grow a few plants and sell their produce, you will develop the confidence to plant more trees and plants and try and make as much profit from it as possible.

Like gardening, you can choose to have your own fishery. You can set up a breeding tank within your home's premise and start breeding fish. You can sell them in bunches and make money out of it. Your initial investment will depend on how much you have at your disposal.

Selling old stuff

You can sell your old and unused stuff on eBay or amazon. You can refurbish them if needed and sell them for a profit. You can also sell your collections if you have a big one. It can be coins, stamps, watches, records etc. there is a market for everything out there. You can simply upload the items and wait for it to be bought. You won't be required to follow up with them and as soon as someone buys your item you will be notified and can quickly pack and sell it.

These form the various ways in which you can raise some extra money on a monthly basis and try and repay all your debts at the earliest. It is possible for you to choose one or more simultaneously as there is no direct participation and make some extra money as well.

Andrew W. Welch

Chapter 7: Saving More Money on a Monthly Basis

In a month, there are just so many places where you can cut down on your spending and save as much money as possible. Here are things that you can do to save a few extra dollars and put it to good use.

Coupons

Start by making use of coupons. Using coupons will help you save on your monthly grocery bills. You can look for coupons in your newspaper or sign up at websites that give away free coupons. You can make a list of things to buy at the beginning of the month and choose a departmental store that accepts coupons. You must use as many as possible and avail a heavy discount. The money that you save can be utilized to pay back the debts that you have or put it into a savings account to use it when you retire. Many people save $100 upwards through couponing and you can match that number if you put your mind to it.

Gifting

Many people decide to gift expensive things to their family and friends. But there is no rule that says you need to always gift something material and so, it is possible for you to gift them a service. This can be to prepare a meal for them or to clean their garden for them etc. By doing so, not only will you strengthen the bond that you share with them but also save on a lot of money on a monthly basis. But if you really must gift something then try buying gifts after the holiday ends and prices are slashed. You can stow them away safely and bring them out next year when it is time to gift. You can possible save between $10 and $50 by doing so.

Electricity

Electricity and telephone bills are two things that you need to take care of in order to prevent disconnection. In the process, you end up paying just so much money that you literally bleed dollars on a monthly basis. The best thing to do to reduce these costs is to make use of renewable sources such as solar and wind power. You can harness these to light a few bulbs and run a few fans in your house. You can also charge your phones and save on your electricity bills. If you have a landline phone that you do not use then have it disconnected immediately. You can save around $5 and $10 by doing this.

Gas bills

Gas bills are also a headache for many people and especially those who are averse to public transport. In order to save money on it, you must buy a car that is fuel-efficient. It is also a good idea to buy an electric car and charge it in your office. You can decide to buy a used car to save on money. Once you start using a fuel-efficient vehicle, you will understand how much money you are saving on a monthly basis and will be motivated to save money in other avenues as well and remain with a lot of money at the end of the month. You can probably save $5 or $10 by taking this up.

Subscriptions

Many people subscribe to books and magazines that they hardly read. It is best to stop subscribing to these and start saving on the money. You must also stop subscribing from club memberships where you hardly go anymore. If you have paid for something like a yoga class then ask if there is a refund policy. You might also have to enquire with other places where you have already paid but are no longer using their service. If they refuse to pay it back then you can start using their services again and not feel guilty about wasting your money. By discontinuing subscriptions you can probably save $100 upwards.

Shop online

It is important to shop online, especially if you are the type that prefers to fill up your cart with unwanted things at the super market. You will have a chance to steer clear of unwanted purchases and not waste your money on unnecessary things. You can also use coupons online and save money on the product that you wish to buy. You can ask someone to suggest the best site that gives away heavy discounts and stick to it. But remember to not leave behind your credit card details, as you might be tempted to buy something and charge it on your card. Choose to go the online banking way instead. It is possible for you to save $15 and $20 by shopping online.

Recycle

You don't have to buy new clothes on a monthly basis. You can choose to recycle your old ones and wear them for another month or two. There are many videos available that show you how you can transform your jeans into skirts, bags, regular tops into tank tops etc. There are also instructional videos for boys and you can look at them and recycle your entire wardrobe. It is also fine to borrow from your sibling's wardrobe as long as you have a chance to save on money on a monthly basis; you can do all the things that feel right. You can possible save $20 to $50 by recycling your clothes.

Do your own grooming

Many people waste money on a monthly basis by hitting the parlor and paying for grooming. But if you do your own nails at home and cut your hair yourself, then you can save on quite a bit of money on a monthly basis. You can probably save around $30 a month and redirect it towards your savings. You can look at instructions available online and get good results every time. You might be slightly shaky in the beginning but will get better with time.

Andrew W. Welch

Chapter 8: Investment Options

Everybody needs to invest his or her money in places where its value can grow. If you are sitting with a lot of money and not putting it to good use then it is best that you look for viable investment options at the earliest. In this chapter, we look at the best options for you and can choose one or two from each category in order to increase your net asset value.

Investments can be broadly classified into three categories, viz. long term investments, midterm investments and short-term investments. These three categories are mainly based on the time that they take to produce results.

Based on the capitalization of the stocks, they can be classified into large cap, mid cap and small cap stocks. These are for equities and we will look at them in detail a little later.

Long term investments

Long-term investments are those that mature in 10 to 12 years. These are investments such as stocks and shares, long-term mutual funds etc.

Stocks/ shares

When a person buys a share of a company, he or she buys into a portion of the profit or loss of that company. So this means that the person is liable to receive a share of the profit the company makes on a quarterly/ yearly basis. Although companies decide to hold these investments for 1 year alone, no investor sells these for at least 10 years. They will not sell the equities owing to receiving good rates of dividend.

Dividend is the profit that people make out of long-term investments. If you look at the face value of the stocks alone then it is not worth it. You need to see how much dividend you receive from the company on a regular basis and collect it into a lump sum.

Long-term investments are for people looking to wait a little and then start earning good profit. It will not be immediate and people have to wait until the company starts a particular project and turns successful. This can take a year, 2 or more depending on the nature of the project.

When deciding to invest in long-term stocks, people need to look at the reputation of the company. It is mandatory to conduct a fundamental analysis and check the company's balance sheet. You need to check the profits they make, the losses they have, the number of investors, total outstanding debt, their stock market graph etc.

Once you are convinced that the company will do well, you can decide to buy a large volume of shares and receive a monthly dividend from the company.

Long term mutual funds

Long-term mutual funds are those where the person invests in mutual funds that take a long time to mature. Mutual funds are schemes where a company collects a lump sum from several people and invests in lieu of them. So a company collects money from several like-minded investors and invests it in the market. This money is compounded. Compounding refers to the interest value being reinvested in the company in order to grow its value. For example: if you invest in the stock market and buy 100 shares of $1000 each for 10 years and earn a dividend of $100 a month. After a year, the company will reinvest this interest into the market in order for its value to grow. So ultimately, the overall value of investment will increase over time.

Business investments

Starting your own line of business is also a long-term investment. You can choose to start a business that will grow in value over a period of time. The business can be related to your field of expertize and you can start one that will turn big over the course of time. So bear in mind what people might like tomorrow and lay the foundations for it today. For example: more and more people are looking to adopt renewable source of energy. So you can decide to start a company that provides people with solar panels or windmills to help in generating energy for themselves. Your business is sure to boom in a matter of a few years. Similarly, choose businesses that will start small but grow big over time. You can also get someone to invest in your business in order to fund the initial capital. If your company then grows big enough, then you can choose to sell shares.

Real estate investments

Real estate is a booming business. All you have to do is buy a house of your choice and rent it out in order to make both a short term and a long-term profit. No property will be valued at the same price over the course of time. And given the growth in population, more and more people will need a place to live at and if you have one on offer then they will flock to occupy it. You can decide to have one or more houses and also try your luck with commercial investments. You will earn a better income if you invest in commercial establishments. The companies will be in a position to pay more rent, which will ultimately result in an increased profit. You can decide to sell your property at any time and make a profit out of it. After depreciation, you might be in a position to sell it for a huge profit, given you have maintained the house and have found the right party to buy it from you.

Precious metals

Precious metals are also a good investment if you are looking for long-term gains. This means that you buy gold and silver and wait for its value to grow. These metals have been regarded as being precious since time immemorial and still continue to be popular with investors. Your gold and silver will rise in value over time and if you sell them at the right time, you will have a chance to break into a large profit. You can choose gold or silver and there is also platinum. The advantage of having this investment is that, the person becomes full owner of the investment. So if you buy 1 kilogram of gold then you are physically handed over that much gold. This is not possible with any other type of investments, except property.

Mid term investments

Mid term investments are those that mature in 5 years' time. This is for all those who are not interested in having their money locked up for 10 years or less than 1 year. Here are some midterm funds that you can choose to invest in.

Midterm mutual funds

Midterm mutual funds are those that mature after 3 years and before 5 years. You can choose this option if you wish to wait for at least 3 years and a maximum of 5 years to see a profit. You just work closely with your fund manager and can check your net asset value at the end of each day. Although you will not be required to take part in the functioning directly, you will have to keep track of your money and make sure that it is being put to good use and you are not headed towards losses.

Foreign currencies

Foreign currencies are the next midterm investment that you can consider for your money. In this, you buy currencies of a foreign country and wait on them to grow in value. Once they do, you decide and sell them off. So buy currencies of countries that are not doing too well in comparison to your local currencies. This will give you a chance to buy them when they are low enough and when they go lower, you will break into a big profit.

Short term investments

Short-term investments are those that are liquidated within a day, week, month, 6 months or a year. So basically, you are not holding on to the investment for a long period of time and giving up its possession at the earliest. This is done in order to make a large profit within a short period of time. That is, the person will have a chance to increase the value of their assets within a short period of time, which is generally 1 year or less. Let us look at these options in detail.

Day trading

Day trading refers to taking a gamble in the stock market. The person looks at certain stocks in the market and invests in them in the morning. He or she will sell the stocks by evening in order to come into a profit. So the person is not holding on to the investment for any more than a day and some might wait for just a week. These are known as day traders and their main aim is to make several small profits in a day. But this type is quite risky as it is not possible to predict how the market will swing. Now say for example: you bought 10 shares of company X at $50 each and 20 shares of company Y for $60 each. At the end of the trading day, X goes up to $60 and you decide to sell it off. You come into a profit of $100 within the course of the day. If the other share's price remains the same then the trader can decide to sell it or hold it if it is set to rise. But if neither rise during the day and start to plummet over the course of the week, then the trader is in big trouble. It is not easy to day trade as there are many things to consider such as the price per share, the fluctuations, news regarding the company etc.

Options

Options are another type of short-term investment that might give away big profits or cause big losses. Now say for example: someone wishes to buy 20 shares priced $50 each which comes to a total of $1000. But they don't have that amount with them and get into a deal with the owner to pay $100 to reserve the shares and then collect it within a 2-week period. Now within these two weeks, if the buyer finds out that the shares are really valuable and that he or she can break into a huge profit by selling it, then the buyer will be lucky and the seller is obligated to sell it at the agreed price. However, if the buyer finds out that the share is actually worthless and is being charged at a marked up value then the buyer can refuse to buy the share but will have to lose the $100 paid as advance.

Bank savings

The next type of investment is bank savings. For many people, this is the safest option as they have a chance to safeguard their money. They can choose to keep their money in the bank and collect an interest on the principle amount on a monthly basis. There are several types of accounts to choose from and the person has to look for the one that pays the best rate of interest. Online accounts are probably the best choice as they will pay you a good rate of interest and you can check your balance online with ease. But the disadvantage is that, you will not get a large sum if you place a small sum with the bank i.e. you need to invest big if you wish to have a big return. So say your profit will be directly proportional to the sum that you place in the bank. Say you place $1000 for a year and the bank pays 2% interest compounded yearly. You will have $1020 at the end of the year. The profit might look really small but your principle sum will remain safe.

Government bonds

Government bonds are the other safe short-term option that people choose. Government bonds are those where a person buy a certain number of shares at a price that is much lesser than its face value. So say a bond is priced at $12 but you get to buy it at $10. The government will issue a bond, pool your money and use it to fund their project. You will be issued a date of maturity for it, after which you can sell your bond at the face value. You will make a small profit there. Here, you need to wait until the maturity period and if you try and withdraw the money any time in between then you will be charged a fine for it. This is not applicable to bank savings and so, is an ideal option for those who find it difficult to keep their money safe and prefer to withdraw from it regularly.

Short cap investments

Short cap investments are those that have a short capitalization. So say there are 1000 shares of a company floating around and are priced at $10 each. The company's market capitalization is 10 X 1000 which is $10000.

Short cap companies are those whose market capitalization is between $300 m and $2000 billion.

Mid cap investments

These will have a market capitalization of between $2 billion and $10 billion.

Long time investments

These companies will have a market capitalization of more than $10 billion.

You can choose to invest where you want depending on how much money and time you have at your disposal. Once you make the investment you need to track it regularly in order to remain aware of where your money is and how it is doing. Once you start investing, you will garner the confidence to expand your portfolio and take newer forms of investments.

Chapter 9: Credit Score Basics

As was mentioned before, everybody needs to borrow money in order to conduct his or her day to day life. It is not possible for someone to lead a luxurious life just by living on his or her income alone. They will require help to buy a car, a house, and a farm etc. and if their credit score is bad, then it won't be possible for them to borrow money for these.

So what is this credit score? Well, credit score refers to the score you are given based on your creditworthiness. Creditworthiness refers to your ability to pay back the debt you have borrowed. All creditors will look for people who will pay them back for sure. If they choose someone who might not be in a position to afford the debt then they will be in trouble.

So it is important for a person to have a good credit score in order to avail credit. Imagine what would happen if you urgently needed a car and nobody is willing to give you money? You will have to look for a very bad car that keeps stopping all the time! So if you have a bad score now then there are tips at the end of this chapter to help you better it. But first, let us look at what ideal credit scores are.

What are ideal credit scores?

720 and above- Excellent

This means that you are in very good position to avail credit from any institution at extremely low interest rates. You are someone that no institution will turn away and will be ready to sanction a loan in no time. This category is extremely hard to reach and even if you do, staying put is next to impossible.

680 to 719- Good

This is a good category but not as good as the previous one. Here too you will receive a loan if they think you are worthy. But you might not get a good rate of interest as you would if you fell in the previous category.

620-679-Average

This is like the cut off line to just making it into the good zone. You will get credit only if you push for your case. Your rate of interest will be high and might have a limit on how much to borrow. A majority of the people fall into this very category.

580-619-Poor

This is a category where it is next to impossible to get credit easily. The institutions might agree but they will levy such a high rate of interest that you won't be able to pay it back even after 10 or 12 years.

500-579-Bad

This is a bad space to be in. the rate of interest charged here would be even higher and you will have to payback an exorbitant amount to the bank.

Less than 500

If you are in this category then forget about getting credit.

What impacts the score?

Many things impact it. Right from how much money you have borrowed in the past to how long it's taken for you to repay it. It also takes into account any defaulting and whether you still have any outstanding credit. It is believed that several card companies purposely add in erroneous entries to bring down the person's credit score. So you need to check your credit report from time to time to see whether yours has some suspicious entries. If you do, then you can approach the creditor to clean up your report.

You can have a free copy of your report by applying for one with any or all three of the credit reporting agencies. These are Equifax, Experian and Trans Union. You might have to wait a few days but once you get the report, analyze it to find out whether it is correct or something extra has been added that is bringing down your final credit score. If you do find something suspicious then be quick to take action and have it rectified at the earliest. If there is no mistake and your score is really bad then here are some things you can do to better it.

How to improve it?

Credit cards

To improve your credit score, start by giving up on your credit cards. It is easy to max out on one and apply for another one. If you keep up with it you will not have any money left with you to carry out day to day activities. The rate of interest they charge is extremely big and thus, you must choose to have just one card and give up the rest. But don't cancel the oldest card that you have. Your oldest card might have a good credit history, which will look good on your report. So try and hold on the oldest and get rid of all the newest ones that you have in your possession.

Similarly, don't cancel cards that still have money in it. If you do, it will show it as having "0" balance which is the same as you maxing out on a card. So don't cancel cards with still money in them. Once you stop making purchases using your credit cards, you will be in a very good position to better your credit report and score alike.

Cash purchases

If you have a big purchase coming up, decide to pay cash for it. Using your card will again mean inviting a heavy interest for the purchase. So make sure you don't get tempted to purchase anything using credit. The same goes for all your online buys. Try and buy using the online banking method and don't pay using your credit card. Remember that you have to cut down on the credit you borrow in order to improve your score. So even if it is a very big purchase like an LCD television, choose to use cash for it that you take from your short-term savings and start saving again.

Limited credit

It is a good idea to make use of a limited credit card. Your bank issues this card and you have to add money into the account yourself. So when you use it as a credit card, you will not incur a big rate of interest. You can add back the money into the account within 60 days. This concept will help you steer clear of unwanted interests and you will have a good chance at improving your credit score.

Small cards

It is always a good idea to buy small cards such as gas station cards and departmental store cards. When you buy them for small amounts and repay them on time, you have a chance at improving your credit scores. So buy these cards and help yourself better your credit report.

Chapter 10: Offbeat Investment Options

When it comes to investments, it will not always be straightforward. You have the option to take a few chances and put your money in off beat avenues. Here are some off beat options for you to try out and increase your money's worth.

Commodities trading

Commodities trading are a good idea for you if you are looking for an offbeat option. Commodities are traded on a daily basis after they are listed in the stock market. All you have to do is choose a few commodities and invest in them. Once their prices rise, the person sells them and comes into a profit. But for this, you have to follow the commodities market closely and understand how it works. You need to check for trends and work on it accordingly. You might have to spend at least 2 months reading about everything and trying to understand what is lucrative and what is not. Ultimately, the idea is to remain with a lot of profit and do away with your debts at the earliest.

Collections

It is a good idea to collect wines, statues, busts, books etc. Anything that will grow in value over time is a good investment. You can choose something that you think will help you convert into a lot of money. The final value of the product will depend on how well you have maintained your collection. So if you wish to take up seriously you need to take good care of it. You need to make sure that it is in its original condition and you have not tampered with it in any way. When you wish to sell it, make sure you keep the documents of authenticity, the original price tag etc. as they will add value to the product.

Auctions

It is also a good idea to take part in auctions and buy rare items at discounted prices. You can then sell these on secondary sites such as amazon or go to an expert to understand its true value and ask to suggest an appropriate collector for it. It is possible for you to make a lot of money by doing this and can also think of setting up an auctioned items business.

Agencies

You can open up agencies such as a travel agency or a tourist guide agency or even real estate agency. By providing these services to people you will have a chance to increase your money's worth. Your agency will thrive if you promote it and get more and more people visit. You can employ someone to carry on the business while you carry on with your day job. If you really do make it big with your side business then you can consider quitting your job and taking it up full time.

Café/ hotel

It is also a good idea for you to start a café or a hotel. This can be your side business. Imagine the amount of money you could make if you had a hotel for yourself. But this will require you to put in some effort into understanding how the café industry works. You can blindly dive nose deep into it, as doing so will only affect your business negatively. So try and gather as much information on the topic as possible before you take it up seriously. Again, once it gains traction, you can quit your day job and take it up seriously.

These are just some of the offbeat investments that you can choose for yourself and increase your money's worth over a period of time. But there can be many more and you need to find out what they are and pursue them.

Chapter 11: Retirement Plans

It is important to have retirement plans in order to have a good life post retirement. If you go into it without having a proper plan then you will have to put up with a lot of troubles and disappointments.

Let us look at some of the plans you need to have in place, in order to remain prepared for your post retirement life.

Insurance

The first thing you need to have is insurance. You cannot decide to remain wary of getting an insurance policy and must get one as soon as possible. You can get one in your 20's itself just to have a good amount waiting lest something goes wrong in your life. You need a policy that fits your needs. You can look at two or three companies and choose the best policy for yourself. You must also have your spouse insured in order to remain on the safer side. If there is any other dependents on you then chose to have their insurance done as well.

Own house

It is mandatory to have your own house by the time you retire. There is no point in living in a rented house for too long. You need to buy yourself a house or construct one for yourself. In fact, I will be great if you have two houses as you can stay in one and rent out the other. You will have a consistent rent coming through which you can save. Just make sure that your house is completely debt free by the time you retire, in order to live without worry and tensions.

Own transport

Public transport might not be a viable option for you once you retire and grow old. So it is also important to have your own transport. You can't rely too much on others to drive you around. So buying a good car is a retirement investment that you must take seriously. You can decide to have two cars and use both in order to have a back up. You can also buy a good quality certified car as your back up car and save on quite a bit of money.

Savings

You must decide and open a retirement savings account as early in life as possible. You must redirect a certain amount towards it on a monthly basis. But make sure you never draw out of it if you haven't retired yet. You need to access it only after your retirement and use the interest that you receive from it. If you started saving really early then you can choose to save the interest money as well and increase your money's worth by a few folds.

But the big question that always gets asked is; how much money is good to save for retirement? Well, this question does not have a standard answer. How much is subjective and depends on how much you wish to have at the end. It will also depend on the type of lifestyle you wish to have post retirement. So a good idea would be to save around $300 to $500 on a monthly basis and redirect it to your retirement savings account. You will be lift with around $144000 by 65 years if you started at age 25. That can be saved at a bank and you can use the interest you receive to fund your everyday life. But this might less for those who wish to live a lavish life. You can choose to invest $500 and upwards in order to have a substantial amount waiting for you at the end.

Parallel income

It is important for you to invest in a passive income that will pay off big by the time you retire. As was said before, you need to start early in order to make good money out of it. Whether it is affiliate marketing or money earned through income, you need to choose something that will pay you returns in the long term. If you are good at something like sewing or knitting or repairing electronics then you can start your own mini business from home. You can choose to invest in two or more businesses simultaneously and set up a good business for yourself.

Portfolio investments

Investment choices that you have for your money was discussed in detail in this book and you can choose something that will work best for you. You need to spread out your portfolio investments and not stick to just one thing. It is best that you aim at receiving a consistent interest month after month and double and triple your investments and earn interests, dividends and other capital gains on a monthly basis.

Future rates

Whenever you plan to save for your retirement, you have to take into consideration the inflated rates that will be waiting for you. So you need to take into account how much money you will need to spend on a daily basis in the future. So say you have to spend

$3000 a month. This might be radically higher than the $1000 that you need to spend now. So bear in mind this price and start saving for the future. There is nothing like "too much" when it comes to saving for your retirement and the more you have, the better.

Community

Remember to always establish a strong sense of community by the time you retire. Even if you are a millionaire, you might urgently need money at a moment's notice, which only a good neighbor can provide. So develop a sense of community and try and have good neighbors when you retire.

Remember that all these will cumulatively help you attain a good amount of money on a monthly basis. You cannot depend on just one thing and need to plan everything out way in advance. There are many people who plan it in such an organized way that they take the option of retiring early. You can do too if you plan everything out carefully and put your money in all the right places.

Andrew W. Welch

Conclusion

I hope you understood the basics of budgeting by now. If used in the right way, budgeting can take care of your finances in a very efficient way. Money management will no longer look like a tedious task if you have a sound budget to back you. You can save more and increase your investment portfolio if you monitor your finances well. You will also be able to reduce your debts and go into a peaceful retirement, if you learn to manage your money well.

I hope you are inspired to track your finances better now. I thank you again for purchasing this book!

Andrew W. Welch

www.ingramcontent.com/pod-product-compliance
Lightning Source LLC
Chambersburg PA
CBHW072307200526
45168CB00014B/885